Work Like You

Twenty Ways to Go From *Meeting* to *Exceeding* Your
Customers' Expectations

★ ★ ★ ★ ★

Bryan K. Williams

★ ★ ★ ★ ★

ENTERPRISE

★ ★ ★ ★ ★
B. Williams Enterprise, LLC
★ ★ ★ ★ ★

We exist to serve others so they may better serve the world. ®

www.bwenterprise.net

www.worklikeyouownit.com

info@bwenterprise.net

Customer Service
Training / Consulting / Products

Contents

A Message from the Author

★ ★ ★ ★ ★

I love customer service. I believe that everyone deserves to receive a caliber of service on par with service at a country club or first-class airline cabin. For a long time, I believed that the only way to build a team of great service providers was for leaders to model the behavior they wanted to see and to hold their staff accountable along the way. Then I began to understand that despite the leaders' best efforts, at some point the front-line staff has to step up, take ownership and work with professionalism. The coach can yell and scream all day, but the players are the ones who must perform with excellence.

The first 14 chapters in this book are a collection of perspectives on how to be the best service professional you can be. The final six chapters are called *Lead Like You Own It*. That section is to help leaders establish the organizational culture necessary to build a team of passionate service professionals.

To help you on your journey, I have included an activity at the end of each chapter.

1. Complete each activity on your own first, to help internalize the secrets, and to apply ways for *you* to improve.
2. Practice the learned concepts until you feel comfortable with them.
3. Lead your team through a discussion around the chapter, and walk them through the same activity.
4. Share your "aha!" moments; talk through how you are working through some of your own challenges...this level of sharing encourages healthy discussion and communicates that you're all in this together.

To Continued Success,

Bryan K. Williams

This book is dedicated to the two ladies in my life.

Lisa and Brylee Reine, I love you.

★ 1 ★

Service Superstars:
Work Like You Own It!

Years ago, when I reported for my first day of work as a restaurant busboy, the maitre'd said something to me that I have never forgotten. He said, "I want you to work in this restaurant like you own it." I remember thinking…"what on earth does he mean by that?"

Not long thereafter, the implication hit me, and I never looked at a job the same again. Working like you own it means you take pride in your work, and will never allow yourself to give anything less than excellence every time. In "The Greatest Bellman I Ever Met," I wrote about a bellman who took immense pride in his job. His service not only made you feel like royalty, but his genuine passion for his job was very obvious. As we continue on our 5-star journey, let us examine the specific qualities that allow such service superstars to shine.

Superstars work like they own it…

- ◆ **Service superstars take pride in their personal appearance**. If you look impeccable, you feel impeccable, and if you feel impeccable, you serve impeccably. It's as simple as that. Although many businesses have a dress code, it is always evident which employees take pride in how they look (regardless if the uniform is a t-shirt & jeans or a suit).

- ◆ **When service superstars begin their shift, the fundamental question they ask themselves is… "How and who will I wow today?"** One housekeeping room attendant took it upon herself to frame the personal pictures of a guest who was staying in the hotel for close to one month. A doorman decided to research and find a book he overheard a guest had been looking for (for several years).

- ◆ A front desk agent ordered a birthday cake for a business traveler who was traveling alone.

- **Service Superstars identify customer preferences, act on them, and share them with teammates.** They know it is not enough for only them to know preferences; they want everyone on their team to know. Whether it's a preferred name or a food/beverage choice, acting on preferences helps to personalize the service experience.

- Superstars give teammates recognition for when they serve with excellence. They love to work with other superstars.

- **Superstars have personal service standards that articulate their individual approach to service.** Whether it is standing up from behind a desk to shake hands, offering to escort a customer, or sending a personal follow-up note card, the personal service standards are a key piece to the service excellence puzzle.

- When they receive a complaint, Superstars take ownership of the complaint, ensure it gets fixed and follows-through until it's resolved (to the customer's satisfaction). They don't hope the customers complain to someone else, and they definitely don't blame other departments. Service superstars take ownership.

Above all, "taking ownership" means you have a vested interest in the business. You make suggestions, you identify common service errors, you take initiative, and you think of innovative ways to attract & retain customers. In short, you are NOT just a warm body taking up space and collecting a paycheck. You are more than that. *You are a service superstar.*

> *Above all, "taking ownership" means you have a vested interest in the business.*

Action Steps

As we all know, it's one thing to plan, but it's another to actually do. So here are 4 easy action-steps to help you work like you own it!

5. Make a list of 3 things to do over the next week to "WOW" your customers. Then make another list of 3 things to "WOW" your team mates. Start "WOWing!"

6. Identify a customer preference, act on it, and share it with your team. Be sure to challenge your team to act on the preference, as well.

7. Recognize a team mate for a job well done. To ensure meaningful recognition, to find out how that specific person likes to be recognized.

8. Write 3 personal service standards and share with your immediate supervisor and your team. Use the personal commitment card for this activity! www.shop.bwenterprise.net

Activity – Work Like You Own It...
What Does That Look Like from Where I Serve?

This activity helps you work through actions that support each Service Super Star Quality commitment.

Instructions

For your position, describe three actions for each Service Superstar quality below. This includes actions, appearance, behaviors, non-verbal communication etc.

Service Superstar Quality	Actions That Support This Quality
Service Superstars take pride in their personal appearance	
When Service Superstars begin their day (shift), the fundamental question they ask themselves is... "How and who will I WOW! Today?"	
Service Superstars identify customer preferences, act on them, and share them with teammates.	

Service Superstar Quality	Actions That Support This Quality
Service Superstars give teammates recognition when they serve with excellence.	
Service Superstars have personal service standards that articulate their individual approach service.	
When they receive a complaint, Service Superstars take ownership of the complaint and make sure it gets fixed…and follows through until it is resolved to the customer's satisfaction.	

★ 2 ★

World~Class Service 101:
Know the Difference Between Meeting and Exceeding Expectations

On a recent trip to an upscale hotel, I had dinner with the restaurant manager. He explained one of the restaurant's main goals was for guests to rate the restaurant a "5," as measured by their guest satisfaction survey. The survey asks guests a series of questions, and each question has a corresponding scale that follows: (1=very dissatisfied, 2=dissatisfied, 3=indifferent, 4=satisfied, 5=very satisfied). The manager told me about all the initiatives he recently implemented to get the **5** rating from guests.

There was a new coffee cup storage system he just implemented to ensure cups are always available for service. Then, there was the cycle-time initiative that tracks the length of elapsed time from the guest's food order being taken to the minute the first course is brought to the table. I told him those initiatives sound good, but none of them would help the restaurant get **5's**. He looked confused. I explained when I order coffee or tea, I EXPECT the beverage to be served on time. When I place my dinner order, I EXPECT the food to be served in a reasonable amount of time (unless I am proactively told otherwise, as in, a well-done steak or a soufflé).

The "4" represents **satisfaction**, which basically means the restaurant did what the guests expected it to do. The staff was friendly...food came on time...everything tasted good...no roaches scurrying around, etc. I went on to explain to get a **5** from a guest, first you must understand what the **5** represents. He really started to listen then. To get a **5** you must not only meet, but exceed expectations. *You can't just put processes and standards in place to avoid messing up. The guest does not expect you to mess up.*

To get a 5 you must not only meet, but exceed expectations.

Instead, actually exceeding expectations and impressing the guest is what leads to a **5**.

Here is a table that illustrates my experience at dinner with the restaurant manager. The "satisfied" column is what really occurred and the "very satisfied" column is what would have made the experience a **5**:

Satisfied (meet expectations)	Very Satisfied (exceed expectations)
Server approaches the table and said "Welcome to XYZ restaurant!"	Use my name in the introduction and welcome me back, if appropriate (note: the host/hostess would have already gotten my name and inquired if I had dined there before)
Server asks if I'm ready to order, then takes my order.	Inquires about my taste preferences and makes menu recommendations using mouth-watering descriptive words and phrases. (e.g., a server in a Fredericksburg, TX restaurant described a beet salad appetizer to me in this way. I ordered it and *loved* it! This was the first time I actually finished eating my beets!)
Asks what drink I want and takes my drink order.	Same as above.
Asks if I would like dessert.	Same as above.
Asks about tea/coffee, and I order tea	Same as above; offers to steep my bag for me.
Says goodbye, thanks for coming.	Offers to call the valet to have my car ready, or offers to call a taxi.

On a recent trip to Portland, Oregon, I visited my client's corporate office for three consecutive days of meetings. Before day 1, the office's administrative assistant emailed me directions to the office from my hotel, along with a link to Google Maps. On day 2 it was raining…a lot. At the end of that day's meetings, I took a short break. When I returned to the meeting room to get my briefcase, there was an umbrella next to it. The administrative assistant anticipated my needs. In fact, I didn't even think of using an umbrella until she left it for me. She provided me with something I didn't even know I wanted!

On day 3, still more rain in Portland, so she brought in a tray of coffee, tea, and hot chocolate to the meeting room. If I was asked about the service experience, do you think that I would rate her service a **5**? You better believe it.

Basically, to get a **5**, you must intentionally do things to get a **5**. You can't just meet expectations and expect customers to rate you as though you exceeded their expectations. The two don't go together.

So, I recommended that the restaurant manager do the following:

1. Work with his team to make a list of all the major service touch points during a typical dining experience (*see table: "Satisfied" and "Very Satisfied"*).

2. Clearly articulate what is "meeting expectations" **(4)** vs. "exceeding expectations" **(5)**.

3. Each day, pick one touch point to focus on. By "focus on" I mean:
   a. Discuss during the pre-shift meetings
   b. Conduct role-plays
   c. Look for opportunities to recognize staff for exceeding expectations for that day's touch point
   d. Encourage staff to recognize each other for exceeding expectation for that day's touch point (I always tell my clients that there is nothing as potent as peer-to-peer recognition).
   e. Every week, challenge staff to come up with more innovative ways to exceed expectations. (Make it fun! Come up with a contest to see who has the most original ideas, etc.).

To sum it up, to get your team to exceed expectations, you must continuously focus on exceeding, expectations. Nothing else will do. Before long, your team's **minimum** expectations of themselves will be to consistently **exceed** the expectations of their customers.

You must continuously focus on exceeding expectations. Nothing else will do

★ 3 ★

World Class Service 102:
Be Memorable...Regardless of Your Job Title

No matter what the job title is, everyone has the power to create memorable experiences for their customers. Regardless of the setting or industry, service excellence begins and ends with at least one person having the desire not just to serve, but to literally improve the life of someone else. While for some, "improve someone's life" may sound like over-reaching,

> *...Service excellence begins and ends with at least one person having the desire not just to serve, but to literally improve the life of someone else.*

think of the days when nothing seems to be going right. Then all of a sudden you go to a grocery store, gas station, or a restaurant and one employee gives a smile, positive eye contact, and treats you like absolute royalty. That one employee just made a profound and memorable impact on you whether you realize it or not.

Recently, I visited a Whole Foods grocery store to see what dinner options they had. I knew from past experiences Whole Foods has buffet stations within the store with various types of cuisine. However, it was my first time visiting that particular location, so I was unsure how the food stations were laid out. Before I could ask for help, I noticed one employee who was stocking shelves. She stopped what she was doing, walked over to me and asked if I needed assistance.

When I asked about the food station locations, she told me she would be happy to give me a tour. I began to think that I had mistakenly walked into the Ritz-Carlton! After giving me a masterful tour and articulately explaining the various food stations. She asked if there was anything further I needed help with. I then asked if they carried a certain brand of drinks; she said she was unsure, but could find out the answer a.s.a.p. She quickly found a colleague to inquire, then came back and happily confirmed they did. She then escorted me to the beverage section where the drinks were.

Now, I don't know about you, but that was the first time in my life that a shelf-stocker provided service to me in such an engaging, self-less, and informative manner. That employee *worked like she owned it!*

She was the exact opposite of a **BM**. A "BM" is a name I use to describe those who do the *bare minimum* in their job. **BM's** do just enough to not get written up, suspended, or fired. BM's have no interest in exceeding expectations. Barely meeting expectations is sufficient. It was clear the Whole Foods employee saw her job as much more than "just a shelf stocker." She understood her main purpose is to make each customer feel valued and to help them find what they are looking for...plus more. She embraced the fact that, in her role, she potentially has the most **touch points** with the customers who are shopping.

Her actions reminded me of a famous quote from Dr. Martin Luther King Jr., which reads, "If a man is called to be a street sweeper, he should sweep streets even as Michelangelo painted, or Beethoven composed music, or Shakespeare wrote poetry. He should sweep streets so well that all the hosts of heaven and earth will pause to say, here lived a great street sweeper who did his job well".

The job doesn't define the person, the person defines the job. At one point in my career, I was the employee dining room (cafeteria) manager for a luxury hotel. While the hotel was luxury, there was nothing **luxury** about the cafeteria. Up to that point a large chunk of my career had been spent working in fine-dining restaurants, so my professional and personal goal was to help transform the cafeteria into a place that all the hotel's employees would be happy and proud to visit.

My team and I treated the cafeteria like a restaurant. In addition to the core duties of maintaining a clean environment and serving nutritious foods, we opened doors for our "guests," helped them carry trays to their tables, and hand-delivered the monthly menu to the hotel departments. In short, we did not allow the common perception of "cafeteria staff" to hinder our passion to provide memorable service to whomever we were fortunate to serve each day.

It is always refreshing to see service superstars with passion, pride and professionalism. If they had a declaration, it would read:

I am passionate about serving others.

I follow up with guest complaints until they are 100% satisfied with the resolution.

I do not blame other departments for service errors.

I consistently look for ways to go above and beyond to delight my customers.

I take initiative and ownership to create memorable experiences for my customers.

I am consistently warm and receptive.

I am not only an ambassador of my company, but of my industry.

I can make my customers feel special by being attentive and eager to serve.

I help my teammates get better.

I always search for ways to improve my service.

I am engaging.

I work like I own it!

For everyone who loves to provide engaging service, regardless of the job title, knowing you made a difference in someone else's life is reward enough. So today, make a commitment that every role you are in will be done with excellence, and more importantly, someone else's life will be better because of how you work like you own it.

Activity – Being Memorable

This activity helps you work through ways in your current role you can be memorable…or helps them set goals for being memorable.

Instructions

Use the table below to list ways you currently (or in the future will) carry out the declarations of a "Work Like You Own It" Service professional:

Think About...	Ways You Do or Will Work Like You Own It...
How am I passionate about serving others?	
What are some ways I follow up with guest complaints until they are 100% satisfied with the resolution?	
What are some ways that I personally own responsibility for service errors?	
In what ways do I go above and beyond to delight my customers?	

Think About...	Ways You Do or Will Work Like You Own It...
What do I do to take initiative and ownership to create memorable experiences for my customers?	
How do I consistently demonstrate a warm and receptive welcome and experience for my customers?	
How do I demonstrate that I am not only an ambassador of my company, but of my industry?	
In what ways do I demonstrate attentiveness and eagerness to serve to ensure my customers feel special?	
How do help my teammates get better?	

Think About...	Ways You Do or Will Work Like You Own It...
In what ways do I search for ways to improve my service?	
What are some behaviors that I demonstrate that engage my customers?	
What are some ways that I demonstrate	

★ 4 ★

5~Star Employees (Part 1)

Chapter 16 in this book is about "5-star leaders". These leaders are committed to only one standard: *Excellence.* They expect nothing less of themselves or from their team. While it is important to describe excellent leadership, it is also important to describe another key piece of the service excellence puzzle…the "5-star employee". Five-star employees are equally passionate with excellence and take great pride in engaging their customers with purpose-driven service. I can still remember the exact moment when I realized there was a difference between an employee and a 5-star employee. At the time, I was a banquet server in a luxury hotel and was given a tray of hors d'oeuvres to serve the guests.

> *Five-Star leaders are committed to only one standard:*
> *EXCELLENCE.*

The chef stopped me before I served the first guest. He asked if I knew what the hors d'oeuvres were and how they were prepared. It became immediately clear that I only had a vague idea of how to describe the items. The chef then looked at me directly in the eyes and said, "You are NOT a professional." Those words forever changed how I viewed service delivery. After that one-sentence from the chef, I went back to the kitchen and thoroughly acquainted myself with each hors d'oeuvres name, ingredients, and preparation. When I returned to the banquet function, I saw the chef, pulled him to the side and thoroughly explained each hors d'oeuvres. He then said "Now, you are a professional."

Being well prepared is the first step to serving with excellence. Five-star employees are consistently well prepared, purpose-driven, and passionate about their work. In fact, over the past several years I've had the good fortune of serving in various capacities and have focused on eight very specific service commitments.

Collectively, they are called "Commitment to Engage My Customers," and are now available on a pocket card exclusively on www.shop.bwenterprise.net.

Here are the first four commitments:

Commitment 1: I will welcome you as if you are a guest in my own home.

Imagine you have a friend you have not seen in a long time. If that friend is coming to visit, you will likely be extremely happy to see them. Your happiness will be obvious through your body language, smile, and tone of voice. The same is true when customers choose to patronize your business. Welcome them! Be eager to serve.

Commitment 2: I will tell you I look forward to serving you and mean it genuinely.

When my wife and I were shopping for our current home, we used to visit various open houses. At one particular open house, the agent was particularly professional and genuinely service-oriented. Even though he must have given dozens of house tours that day, we felt like we were the first tour he gave.

**Tip: Customers don't care how many hours you have worked today. Each customer wants (and deserves) to feel like their experience with you is unique and fresh...not commercialized and stale.

Each customer wants (and deserves) to feel like their experience with you is unique and fresh...

Even though we were not yet ready to select an agent, he said he looked forward to serving us. Not long thereafter, we selected that agent and it was a wise choice. He would regularly say "I am at your service" or that he looked forward to seeing us.

Commitment 3: I will create a total experience by anticipating your needs.

The customers' total experience is made up of several touch points. Five-star employees who take pride in anticipating their customers' needs can enhance each touch point. At a recent dinner in Spain, the server thanked us for dining at his restaurant and subsequently gave my wife three roses. Nice touch! After returning to the room, my wife laid the roses in front of the bathroom mirror so she could admire them during the remainder of our stay at the hotel.

The very next day, we went for a walk and when we returned to the room, the room attendant had carefully clipped the rose stems and placed them in a nice vase. Those two simple gestures added tremendous value to our hotel stay. Interestingly, I always tell people that it usually does not cost anything extra to create an exceptional memory for their customers.

That room attendant paid attention, took action, and created a lasting memory.

Commitment 4: I will tell you it was a pleasure to serve you, and invite you back.

Having the opportunity to serve others is a privilege and should not be taken lightly. Five-star employees have a great habit of thanking their customers for the opportunity to be of service. Not only do they thank their customers, but 5-star employees also articulate how much they wish to be of service to those customers in the near future. I have been to a few restaurants that have a great process to enliven this particular commitment. Whenever guests are leaving the restaurant, the staff closest to the exit, stop whatever they are doing and give a gracious goodbye to the departing guests. They thank the customers for visiting and invite them back.

**Tip: This same process, or some variation of it, can be applied in any business.

Be a 5-Star employee and use these commitments to engage yourself, your co-workers, and your customers. Focus on one commitment every day and think of specific ways to provide engaging service to every customer. If you catch someone on your team providing engaging service, genuinely *thank them!*

Write a thank you card or give some other type of personalized recognition. As I've written in previous chapters, to get excellence, you must focus on excellence. There is nothing more powerful than 5-star employees encouraging each other. Be well-prepared…be purpose-driven…and be passionate about giving engaging service.

Activity – How to Be a 5-Star Employee

This activity will help you and if applicable, your team identify and agree on actions and behaviors needed to meet each necessary commitment for being a 5-Star Employee.

Instructions

Use the provided space to outline actions or behaviors that will help you and/or your team meet each commitment.

My Commitment...	How I Will Meet It...
Commitment 1: I will welcome you as if you are a guest in my own home.	
Commitment 2: I will tell you that I look forward to serving you and mean it genuinely.	
Commitment 3: I will create a total experience by anticipating your needs.	
Commitment 4: I will tell you that it was a pleasure to serve you, and invite you back.	

★ 5 ★

5-Star Employees (Part 2)

Recently, I called a well-known hotel and asked for the concierge desk. Although I was not a guest at the time, I previously stayed at this particular hotel chain several times prior, and considered myself to be a loyal customer. The reason I called was to merely get some quick restaurant recommendations. The concierge advised me that since I was not a guest, she could not assist. Even after I advised her that I am a loyal guest and have stayed at the company's hotels several times before, she repeated her stance.

Sure she may have been doing what she was told by her supervisor, or perhaps she was unaware of how easy it would have been to make some recommendations (after all, she could have also recommended the restaurant in her own hotel). Maybe she just didn't care. That same concierge could have said she would be happy to assist and inquired if I was celebrating a special occasion. She then could have made a few recommendations and offered to give me the phone number of the restaurants. The latter approach would have reinforced my expectations of the hotel chain and created more opportunities for me to refer others. In 5-Star Employees Part 1, I wrote about four commitments that world-class service employees share. Here is the fifth commitment:

Commitment 5: I will make you feel special, included, valued, and appreciated.

The concierge I wrote about did not understand that EVERY customer is priceless. The provision of engaging service should be inclusive and just as important for those who are "potential" customers. Commitment 5 means 5-star employees must look for every single opportunity to win the hearts of current *AND* potential customers.

Any customer who is in the vicinity of a 5-star employee should feel his or her passion to serve. Let's assume I go to a shopping mall and walk into a retail store. I then ask the store employee for directions to the food court.

The eagerness of that employee to assist may cause me to return to that store to shop and possibly refer it to others in the future.

Here is another scenario to enliven Commitment 5. If I accompany my uncle to the doctor's office, and the doctor's staff is engaging and kind to me as well, then I might return for personal services. If I visit a church with a friend, and the ushers, staff, and congregation are welcoming, then I might be more likely to return. The point is EVERYONE is a customer, because everyone has the potential to return and refer others. So if you serve in a business that is dependent on tourism dollars, be just as service-oriented to the locals (if not more). If you serve in a retail environment, be just as engaging to "window shoppers;" be kind to those who express no desire to patronize your business at the current moment…your kindness and engaging demeanor may eventually change their mind.

EVERY customer is priceless!

This particular commitment also has additional relevancy to the current economic climate. I regularly see many businesses that are literally throwing money out the window. For many businesses, revenue is not lost solely because of a recession; it may be lost because customers choose not to patronize those businesses. That's right…many times it's a consumer choice to avoid certain businesses because the staff does not make consumers feel special, included, valued, and appreciated. For example, over the last six months, most decisions I've made to avoid booking a flight with a particular airline, dining at a certain restaurant, or staying in a hotel had nothing to do with a recession. Those decisions had everything to do with employees giving apathetic service. The point here is many businesses use "the economy" as a scapegoat for their organization's woes, when all they may need is to re-focus on the customer. Five-star employees understand this premise. To them, every customer is priceless.

If you are a manager and you are reading this, please ensure your 5-star employees are surrounded by other 5-star employees. These employees yearn to work with team mates who care like they care…who push like they push…and who serve like they serve. From a 5-star employees' perspective, there is nothing better than giving 5-star service in a 5-star organization run by 5-star leaders.

Activity – How to Be a 5-Star Employee

This activity will help you and if applicable, your team identify and agree on actions and behaviors needed to meet each necessary commitment for being a 5-Star Employee.

Instructions

Use the provided space to outline actions or behaviors that will help you and/or your team meet the commitment.

My Commitment...	How I Will Meet It...
Commitment 5: I will make you feel special...	
Included.	
Valued.	
Appreciated.	

★ 6 ★

5-Star Employees (Part 3)

In two previous chapters, we discussed the influence that 5-star employees have on their guests, their team, and their company. These 5-star employees take immense pride in their jobs and refuse to settle for anything less than giving exceptional service. In Chapter 4, we reviewed four commitments 5-star employees have in common. Then in Chapter 5, we discussed exclusively the fifth commitment. In this chapter, we will review the remaining 3 commitments and conclude with the mantra of a 5-star employee.

Commitment 6: I will tell you I am happy to see you, and I am happy to serve you.

This commitment shows your "eagerness to serve." Even if you don't actually say "I am happy to see you and serve you," your actions should. I accompanied my wife on a recent trip to a cosmetics store, and the entire staff did a marvelous job of enlivening this commitment. EVERY employee gave eye contact, smiled, and welcomed us. There was no question that their primary purpose was to provide us with a memorable shopping experience.

Commitment 7: I will make sure you are happy you have chosen us instead of our competitors.

All things being equal, guests prefer to patronize businesses that make them feel special and appreciated. Actually, it is the people within those businesses that make customers feel special and appreciated. Five-star employees understand guests have a choice regarding where to spend their hard-earned money. Five-star employees recognize every service touch point and consistently make deposits at each touch point.

> *Five-Star employees understand guests have a choice regarding where to spend their hard-earned money.*

Commitment 8: I will earn your patronage, your referrals, and your loyalty.

The key word in this commitment is "earn." Earning your guest's loyalty is a team effort. Every person must make significant contributions. However, it is important to note that your individual actions are critical to the team's success.

Five-star employees constantly evaluate their service with the following question: Why will guests remember the service I provided?

On a recent trip to the beautiful Shawnee Inn and Golf Resort in the Pocono Mountains, I met several 5-star employees. One morning I ordered breakfast through room service, and I fully expected a server to bring my meal to the room (as usual). To my surprise, the meal was delivered by two cooks. Both of them arrived at my room and expressed their gratitude to me for staying at the resort. The cooks even proceeded to explain each dish and how it was prepared. *Memorable.* Their act helped to earn my patronage, referrals, and loyalty. It is amazing to see a true 5-star employee at work. They are passionate, committed, and hospitable all at the same time.

Imagine if 5-star employees had a declaration…it would read:

★ ★★ ★ ★ **I Am a 5-Star Employee** ★ ★★ ★ ★

I am passionate about serving others.

I follow-up with guest complaints until they are fully satisfied with the resolution.

I do not blame other departments for service errors.

I consistently look for ways to go above and beyond to delight my guests.

I take initiative and ownership to create memorable experiences for my guests.

I am consistently warm and receptive.

I am not only an ambassador of my company, but of my industry.

I can make my guest's stay very special by being attentive and eager to serve.

I help my teammates get better.

I always search for ways to improve my service.

I am engaging.

I am a 5-Star Employee.

Activity – How to Be a 5-Star Employee

This activity will help you and if applicable, your team identify and agree on actions and behaviors needed to meet each necessary commitment for being a 5-Star Employee.

Instructions

Use the provided space to outline actions or behaviors that will help you and/or your team meet the commitment.

My Commitment...	How I Will Meet It...
Commitment 6: I will tell you that I am happy to see you, and that I am happy to serve you.	
Commitment 7: I will make sure you are happy that you have chosen us instead of our competitors.	
Commitment 8: I will earn your patronage, your referrals, and your loyalty.	

★ 7 ★

World-Class Service:
What if Every Employee Served Like a Concierge?

Employees often feel constrained by their job titles. Doormen should mainly open doors, massage therapists should mainly give massage treatments, and room attendants should mainly clean rooms. This type of constraint can inhibit the potential creativity and zeal that employees experience in their jobs. I've held close to 20 different roles in the hospitality industry, ranging from busboy to corporate training director, but only one role truly allowed me to "break free." In the role, my job description was to move heaven and earth to delight every guest all the time. That role was as a concierge. I loved that job.

Being a concierge was purely about anticipating, organizing, and delivering exceptional service. Even after I moved on to other roles, including my current one as a service consultant, I approach every customer with the same concierge mindset… "I will do whatever it takes to provide the best service you have ever received."

Being a concierge is purely about anticipating, organizing, and delivering exceptional service.

On a recent trip to Spain, I stayed at the Hotel Puente Romano in Marbella. My interactions with the lobby concierge were exceptionally positive and I began to wonder, "What would happen if every employee in a business developed that same concierge mindset? What if every employee served like a concierge and did not allow their service delivery to be constrained by their job title?"

If this becomes the case in your business, here is what each employee, including yourself, needs to do consistently:

- **Never say "no."** Always give options and alternatives.

- Going above and beyond is the minimum standard of performance for all customers.

- **Feel empowered to create exceptional memories**. This assumes your leader trusts you enough to empower you, coach (not chastise) your efforts, and regularly give encouragement.

- Coordinate and work with other departments to surprise and delight customers. It is difficult to go above and beyond by yourself.

- Always follow through on customer requests.

Note: *If you are a senior leader, please ensure every employee knows their primary job is to serve customers. Each employee should know this from the very beginning during the recruitment and interview processes. If you are managing a grocery store, even your employees who stock shelves should know their primary role is to help the customer find everything they want and their secondary role is to stock shelves. That message MUST be communicated to all employees at all levels.*

When I was a restaurant server, I enjoyed talking with my guests and learning about their preferences. One night I was listening to a vacationing couple tell me about their favorite types of foods. They happened to love fresh mangos. They also wanted to visit a few good local restaurants before their vacation ended. I immediately checked with the hotel kitchen staff to see if there were any fresh mangos in stock; unfortunately they were all out. Before returning to work the next day, I empowered myself to stop at a local grocery store to pick up a few fresh mangos for the guests. When I got to work, I coordinated with the chef and a room service employee to make a special tray of freshly cut mangos for the guests. This tray was sent to the room via room service, along with a hand-written note from me. The note also contained a list of very good local restaurants.

I then followed up with the concierge team, who sent a copy of the local restaurants' menus to the guest's room. The following day I contacted the guest to find out about their restaurant experience and to see if there was anything else I could to make their stay a memorable one. I was not constrained by my job title. I was fortunate to work in an establishment where the senior leaders expected, encouraged, and rewarded such behavior.

Make it a point to encourage yourself and your team to break free. You are more than a job title, you are a service professional. It does not matter what industry you are in. As long as you have customers, you are in the *service business.* World-class concierges take great pride in orchestrating memorable service experiences for their guests. With a concierge mindset, every employee on your team will surely excel at engaging their customers every day.

It does not matter what industry you are in. As long as you have customers, you are in the service business.

Activity – What if Every Employee Served Like a Concierge?

The true declaration of a concierge is... "I will do whatever it takes to provide the best service you have ever received." Building a "concierge culture," both individually and as a team, requires making decisions about how you serve your customers.

Instructions

Answer the questions below to help identify ways in which you can provide the best service your customers have ever received...

1. What are some barriers you currently experience in your job that prevent you from providing world-class service?

_____

_____

_____

2. How can you address them?

Personally?	With Your Supervisor?	Within Your Culture?

3. What are some things you can do to perform outside of your role to deliver world-class service?

_____

_____

4. What other departments can you work with to orchestrate a "WOW!" experience?

_____

_____

5. Choose a service or product that your company does not provide, but for which customers often ask you. Instead of saying "No," what were some options / alternatives?

_____

_____

★ 8 ★

Delivering World-Class Service: Personal Service Standards

Escort guests rather than pointing out directions...Never say "it's not my job..." Answer the phone with a smile...These are all examples of service standards. Companies use them to train their staff. Even while having service standards, for service to become truly a way of life, such standards must be embraced by each individual on the team. *I* must want to escort guests...*I* must want to answer the phone in 3 rings, and *I* must want to offer assistance if a customer appears lost. So in addition to your company-wide standards, challenge your individual employees to think of ways they intend to contribute to your company's service mission. These "personal" service standards are unique to the individual, should reinforce their strengths, and permit them to address their opportunities for improvement.

These "personal" standards are unique to the individual.

A few personal service standards I've seen are:

- ◆ "I will always think of ways to exceed expectations."
- ◆ "I will follow up with all customers within 30 minutes."
- ◆ "I will make each customer feel truly unique."
- ◆ "I will find out something interesting about every customer in order to personalize the service."

Like goals, it's good to write personal service standards down, look at them daily, and share them. Communicate the personal service standards with your co-workers and manager. They can help hold you accountable to meeting those standards and vice versa.

If you are a manager, I recommend you do the following:

1. Begin with yourself. Write your own personal service standards. This is a critical step.

As Gandhi said, "Be the change you want to see in the world". Plus it can seem hypocritical to ask your staff to do something you are not doing.

2. Lead a meeting or training session on service excellence and why it is important for the team. Explain that providing engaging service is what each employee should commit to doing every day.

3. Share your own personal service standards with your team, and then ask them to help hold you accountable for meeting those standards. Explain that you will do the same for them. After all, service excellence is a team effort.

4. Instruct your team members to write their individual personal service standards. Encourage them to write specific behaviors.

5. Key Step: Have employees share their Personal Service Standards with you (their manager) or their immediate supervisor…success is not something you do in the future…otherwise one would never get there.

6. Keep a file (paper or electronic) that contains each person's personal service standards.

7. In daily interactions, ask individual employees to share their personal service standards with you. Also ask them how they intend to use at least one of the standards that day.

8. During your routine one-on-one meetings (which you should have), review your employee's personal service standards, and provide feedback regarding their performance against those standards.

To assist you, I have developed a pocket-sized card for you to easily write your personal service standards. *Visit my company store at www.shop.bwenterprise.net to order this card.*

There is also space to write the "purpose" of your role. Please refer to the *Function vs. Purpose* article to refresh your memory. This card also features personal commitments that have been adapted from *EngageMe…the Voice of Your Customer.*

As you finish reading this chapter, commit to writing your own personal service standards. Even if you already provide exceptional service, your personal service standards will serve as inspiration for everyone else. A great hotel executive once told me that success is not something you do in the future...otherwise one would never get there. Success is what you do today, in this very moment, and everyday thereafter. Writing your personal service standards today will assist with your commitment to excellence, and your commitment to engage every customer with your service.

> *...success is not something you do in the future...otherwise one would never get there.*

Activity – From Where I Serve

This activity and ongoing one-on-ones will help start or continue rapport between you and your team as you both deliver world-class service. The key to success is to design your routine in such a way that delivering service excellence is a natural part of each day.

Instructions

1. Use the template below to write your own personal service standards.
2. If you supervise a team of service professionals, lead a meeting to:
   - Discuss and gain agreement on how important service excellence is to your team, company, and business
   - Provide examples for how to deliver service excellence within each role
3. Provide a copy of the template below, and ask each member of your team to write their own personal service standards *and* behaviors / actions that support them.
4. Set up one-on-one meetings with each member of the team to discuss and agree on Personal Service Standards for each respective role.
5. Work together to integrate these standards into their Performance Plan / Process.
6. Continuously observe and follow-up; then coach and recognize when the standards are demonstrated.
7. Give team members opportunities to share their own stories of how their standards positively impact the customer.

My Personal Service Standard	Why It Is Important...	How It Impacts My Customer

★ 9 ★

Make Each Touch Point Memorable: Cha-Ching!

A few years ago, I wrote an article entitled Engage every customer, one touch point at a time. The basic message was the entire customer experience is comprised of several touch points. A touch point is any interaction between a customer and your business. For each touch point, you either make a deposit or a withdrawal. More deposits equals more customer engagement, and more withdrawals equals less engagement. Pretty simple right? I even have a client whose employees give a cheer whenever someone makes a deposit... "Cha-Ching!" I couldn't stop smiling after I heard that one.

A touch point is any interaction between a customer and your business.

I would like to revisit the touch points idea, because delivering a memorable service experience truly comes down to the deposits individual employees make. Service superstars are deeply committed to not only making deposits, but they are always looking for ways to make each touch point memorable. Allow me to give you four recent examples.

◆ *Example 1:* Just recently, I checked into a hotel in Oklahoma, and as I approached the elevator a bellman was just coming out of the same elevator. When he saw me, he immediately turned around and held the door open for me. He then wished me a pleasant stay.

◆ *Example 2:* In a hospital in Texas, one nurse, in particular, always asks her inpatients if they are expecting any visitors that day. If visitors are expected, the nurse takes it upon herself to get additional chairs and water before the visitors arrive. She even asks for their names beforehand so she can properly address them.

- *Example 3:* After speaking at a convention, one of the organizers asked what time my flight was. After I told him, he offered to personally drive me to the airport instead of having me take a taxi. He wanted to make sure I received a gracious goodbye as opposed to taking a cab back to the airport.

- *Example 4:* At a breakfast omelet station, the chef took my order and proceeded to make my omelet. After preparing it, he actually walked from behind his station and brought the plate to my table. He also thanked me for the opportunity to be of service.

For those of you who are thinking of the productivity time he lost, the process of walking me to the table was less than one minute, and it created a memorable experience for me.

- *Example 5:* I was returning a rental car back to the airport, and I was very late for my flight. The rental car attendant said the obligatory, "good afternoon, how are you today?" When I replied that I was late, she said, I'll be happy to drive you over to your gate…jump in the passenger seat!" Wow. I definitely did not expect that.

Those examples merely illustrate that enhancing each touch point does not have to be expensive…or cost any money for that matter. All it requires is a team of employees who consistently *work like they own it.* Pay attention to the word "consistently"…I will come back to it in a minute. I am confident everyone reading this has heard the term, "world-class" before.

Businesses make promises to provide world-class service to their customers. Restaurants boast of having world-class chefs, and even hospitals proclaim to have a world-class medical team. What does it really mean? A quick look in the dictionary and an online search say that world-class means, "to be ranked or considered among the world's best."

Makes sense, but how do you get there? How do you become considered among the world's best, regardless of your job or industry? Before I answer that question, allow me to share a recent service experience with you. I called a company and the phone rang five times before the operator answered, "How can I provide world-class service today?"

Interesting. My curiosity was peaked, so I was eagerly anticipating the world-class experience. What followed was anything but world class. The operator cut me off mid-sentence at least 3 times and then transferred me without saying she would do so. That's not world-class, is it?

Even if that particular operator provided excellent, memorable and outstanding service, that would NOT be world-class. World-class is primarily about one word...*consistency.*

Being excellent is not enough...you have to be consistently excellent. Being memorable is not enough...you have to be consistently memorable. Being engaging is not enough... you have to be *consistently* engaging.

World-class means you are "on" every day, regardless of your personal or professional circumstances. Being a service professional means you do what you are supposed to do, when you are supposed to do it, whether you feel like it or not. You have probably noticed this world-class thing requires lots of hard work...you're right! It is not easy, otherwise EVERYBODY would be world-class. It requires consistent effort, and that effort is what separates good from great and great from world-class.

So make a commitment today to engage your team in a discussion about touch points. Identify all the key touch points in your department, and then brainstorm ways to enhance each touch point. Make each touch point memorable! Put the touch points and their enhancements on a bulletin board, then focus on one touch point per week (per day is even better). As I always say, serving others is a privilege and your customers deserve the very best you and your team have to offer. Before long, you will hear your team (and cash registers) go Cha-Ching!

Activity – Make Each Touch Point Memorable: Cha-Ching!

This activity helps teams collectively discover the importance of touch points. Once discovered, teams can then identify and agree on ways to enhance them.

Instructions

1. Meet with each member (or functional group) within your team.
2. Discuss the meaning of touch points as explained in this chapter.
3. Stress the importance of treating each service opportunity as a privilege.
4. For each role, and from start to finish, list all the touch points you are privileged to share with your customers. Use the template below to get started.
5. Type up the touch points for each role…enlist the help of creative members of your team to make this a fun and engaging presentation.
6. Place the touch points on the employee bulletin board.
7. Identify one touch point per day as the focus for each role within your team.
8. Continuously add to the list as you and your team, through practice, learn more about touch points.
9. Use every opportunity to recognize and reward super-star performance.

Role:
Touch Points

★ 10 ★

Service Ambassadors:
The Key to Providing World-Class Service

It's amazing who some business owners and managers allow to represent their company. On a recent trip, I stopped at a sandwich shop to order some lunch. After the employee told me they were out of the sandwich I had ordered, I asked for her menu recommendation; to which she promptly replied "None of the sandwiches here!" Wow. Perhaps it did not occur to her that by suggesting one of her company's sandwiches, I may actually enjoy it, return, and potentially refer others…all of which translate into additional revenue (plus more job security).

To customers, the person serving them *IS* the company. That employee's actions, words, and everything in between are a direct reflection of the company. In general terms, an ambassador is someone who represents

> *To customers, the person serving them IS the company.*

something or someone. For example, the U.S. ambassador to Brazil is the chief representative of the U.S. in Brazil. This means everything the ambassador does and says is a reflection of the U.S. When Brazilians see the ambassador, they are actually seeing the U.S. The ambassador *IS* the U.S. Whether you like it or not, you *are* the company for which you work. Your customer does not care what department you work in or how long you have been working there. All your customers know is you are an employee. Therefore, you should be an advocate of the business.

I cringe when employees refer to their place of employment as "they" or "them." You are the company, so who exactly is "they" or "them?" On a recent trip, I stopped at a well-known airline's ticket kiosk to print my boarding pass. As I approached the kiosk, three of the ticket agents were embroiled in a heated discussion about an extremely important and critical topic…their work schedules for the next week. For the entire 3-5 minutes I was at the kiosk, not one ticket agent stopped their debate to offer assistance (let alone acknowledge that I existed).

Toward the end of my time at the kiosk, one employee finally removed herself from the employee discussion, and asked if I was checking luggage. I thought for a moment, and decided to keep the bag with me. She then said, "Good, because I wouldn't give them any more money than I had to. Have a nice day." Again…wow.

A culture of world-class service flourishes when your entire team has a sense of ownership. As a leader, be sure to instill that feeling of personal ownership in every employee beginning at the recruitment phase, and on through the remainder of the onboarding process. Tell employees their presence and contributions matter. They should know their team is (and will be) better because of the talents they bring.

A culture of world-class service flourishes when your entire team has a sense of ownership.

Of course, all this talk of having ambassadors also means your company must be worthy of being represented. Is your business a place where people are proud to work and to represent? Why or why not? Being an ambassador is an esteemed position that should not be taken lightly. Each action at every touch point has specific consequences (both positive and negative). So if you are a manager, ensure everyone on your team is a great representative. From sandwich shops to spas to hospitals to hotels, world-class service begins with ambassadors. Ambassadors who are proud of their company and eager to provide exceptional serve with consistency and conviction.

Supplemental section for leaders

The best way for leaders to build a team of ambassadors is to be a shining example of how ambassadors are supposed to act. Beyond being a role-model, here are four practical tips for leaders to implement:

- **Set high performance and service standards** – Be clear about what those standards are. Give vivid examples as needed.

- **Communicate those standards** – Use multiple resources to communicate standards (e.g., pre-shift meetings, newsletters, email signature blocks, screen savers, bulletin boards, daily voice mail, etc.)

- **Give performance feedback** – This is one of the biggest opportunities for improvement amongst leaders. Your team needs to know how they are performing in both good and bad times.

- **Reward excellence** – Be careful how you reward performance. I've seen many managers celebrate when performance expectations are simply *met*. It is fine to acknowledge when expectations are met, but reserve your praise and celebration for when expectations are surpassed (or at least consistently met).

Activity – I Am a Service Ambassador

This activity helps identify barriers that prevent you and if applicable, your team as a whole, from delivering world-class service.

Instructions

1. Using the scale below, rate your actions as a Service Ambassador.
2. If you lead a group, also rate your team as a whole on their actions as a Service Ambassador.
3. Ask your team as a whole, to rate their actions as a Service Ambassador.

1	Never
2	Sometimes
3	Almost Always
4	Always

4. Once all participants have completed the assessment, calculate and share the results.
5. Make plans (as an individual) or gain agreement (as a team) on how:
   - Identify improvements needed (empowerment, tools, etc.) or barriers to remove.
   - Communicate, communicate, and then communicate again, the standards for service ambassadorship.
   - Provide (or seek) feedback throughout each day.
   - Reward and recognize excellence when you see it (as a leader and as a teammate).

Service Ambassador Attributes	1	2	3	4
I Represent the company. I take personal responsibility for being a positive representation of our company to my customers.				
I Recommend the best ways to enjoy our service experience with our customers. I take ownership in the customer experience; I have the inside scoop on ways to best enjoy your visit with us.				
I Reach out to ensure each customer with whom I come in contact enjoys a 5-star experience. I am your host and will do whatever it takes to make you feel like an insider, the most VIP customer we serve.				

Service Ambassador Attributes	1	2	3	4
I Rescue any experience that is not 5-star. Through proactive service, I take responsibility for any part of your experience that is not 5-star. I will do whatever it takes to turn your experience around to exceptional.				
I Recognize that my customers have a choice; I share warm, sincere appreciation when customers choose us! I know you are the reason we open our doors every day; I will help you realize you made the right choice through a warm thank you and sincere appreciation for your business.				

★ 11 ★

The Greatest Nurse I Ever Met

This is my "thank you" to the great nurses of the world. You are a gift to everyone who is fortunate to be served by you.*

I love exceptional customer service…Everything about it! I love that those who serve do not think of themselves as servants, but as service professionals. They enjoy making others feel special. They go out of their way to "WOW." For these service superstars, service is not what they do; it is "who they are." This is why I cringe when I hear healthcare professionals say "I didn't go to school to serve people." Huh? Yes…I've heard that exact quote several times. Hospitality means to take care of others, and guess what the root word is in hospitality. You guessed it…hospital. I firmly believe that healthcare IS the highest form of hospitality. As a healthcare provider, the ENTIRE purpose of your job is to help, assist, empathize and take care of others. All those words mean to serve. Of course, not everyone is meant to serve other people. We have all seen those individuals. That's fine if you don't like to serve…just get a job that doesn't require you to serve. If everyone is not meant to serve, then even fewer people are meant to be healthcare providers. Other people (especially inpatients) are completely dependent on you.

For these service superstars, service is not what they do; it is "who they are."

This brings me to The Greatest Nurse I Ever Met. This nurse works in a hospital in Annapolis, MD, where my cousin was an inpatient for almost two months. I visited him frequently over that two-month period and saw the care he received firsthand. Though most of my training and consulting clients are in the healthcare industry, I must admit this was the first time that I truly "felt" and understood just how important nurses are. From my perspective, they account for the vast majority of the patient service experience. The physician would do her rounds in the morning and might spend 5 – 7 minutes with my cousin, then leave.

It was the nursing team who supervised and administered the healthcare for the rest of the day. It was the nurses who were called if my cousin needed something. It was the nurses who listened when he had an immediate concern. If the hospital is a building, then the nurses are the heart and soul of that building.

One of my favorite books is *If Disney Ran Your Hospital,* in which I read an interesting quote, "Hospitals don't have patients, doctors do". That powerful statement is true in many cases. However, I can now see how offensive that statement can be to nurses who build enduring relationships with their patients and patients' families. Nurses cry, laugh, and spend time with their patients all-day, every day.

So during my cousin's inpatient stay, one exceptional nurse was Stacy. Besides her exceptional clinical acumen, her warmth and eagerness to serve seemed just as potent as any medication given to my cousin. As an inpatient, he was fortunate to have received multiple flowers for his room. After a few days, he ran out of vases to put them in, so Stacy said, "I'll make you one!" She quickly returned with a disposable Styrofoam water pitcher and cut the top off to make an impromptu flower vase. I refer to that as a touch point deposit, and when there are deposits, I say Cha-Ching!

Stacy didn't stop there. Since my cousin knew he would be in the hospital for at least a few months, he asked for some good places in the surrounding area to order food that could be picked up or delivered. She could have easily referred him to the hospital's concierge, but that would go against her service ethics. Stacy is a nurse who "works like she owns it," so she gave him a hand-written list of her favorite restaurants and next to each restaurant, she noted the approximate distance from the hospital and type of cuisine. She even put a star next to the ones she really liked. *Cha-Ching!*

Each week, the inpatients receive a menu of food offerings from the hospital's cafeteria. Since Stacy knew my cousin would be staying for a while, she got him a menu for the entire month. *Cha-Ching!*

When Stacy entered the room each day she beamed, "Good Morning Sunshine! So here's the plan for today." Being in a potentially depressing situation as my cousin was, it was refreshing to have an upbeat, positive personality to take the edge off being confined to a hospital bed for an extended period of time. *Cha-Ching!* After his daily bed bath, Stacy would get him a warm towel and change his bed sheets using warm sheets and blankets. *Cha-Ching!*

In short, Stacy made him feel like he was her only patient. She never complained or talked about her workload or how many patients "they" gave her. She never complained about her bosses, co-workers, or the hospital (at least not in my presence, or within earshot). In fact, she was one of the only nurses we did *not* hear bad-talking or gossiping in the hallway. Yes, patients can hear everything said in the hallway. In fact, she beamed about the hospital; only spoke positively and even bragged about the hospital's expansion plans. That is being a true ambassador.

So, Stacy is the greatest nurse I ever met, and I'm sure there are several more "Stacy's" in the world. As an observer of Stacy's caregiving, I felt privileged to have seen her in action, and I am sure she is humbled that she gets to do what she loves to do every day...and get paid for it. Service is not what she does, service is who she is.

...she beamed about the hospital; only spoke positively and even bragged about the hospital's expansion plans. That is being a true ambassador.

Activity – Growing and Developing "Stacy's"

This activity will help you get started on either growing a *"Cha-Ching!"* culture within your existing team…or begin creating that culture.

Instructions

1. During the last few activities, we have identified, agreed on, and observed actions and behaviors that help deliver a "5" experience. These "5's" have resulted not just from actions, but from attitudes.

2. For each function on your team, list the attitudes (core competencies) that you need to help consistently deliver a "5" experience to your customers. In other words, what would Stacy "look like" if she was a member of *your* team?
   We have included some competencies that Stacy demonstrated to help you get started.

3. Use this list to:

   ◆ Identify development opportunities for members of your team who do not currently or consistently demonstrate "Cha-Ching" behaviors.

   ◆ Create a new-hire profile for someone who would be a fit for your team's aggressive "Cha-Ching" culture.

Attitude/Behavior...	What it "Looks Like" on My Team...
Builds Strong Relationships	
Exceptional Job Skills	
Warm/Friendly/Eager to Serve	
Uses available resources to "WOW!" customers	
Think & acts like a Concierge (*see Chapter 7*)	
Works like they own it	
Always demonstrates an upbeat, positive personality	

Attitude/Behavior...	What it "Looks Like" on My Team...
Helps each customer feel like they're the *only customer*	
Is a true Ambassador of the Brand	
Never Complains	
Never Gossips	
Service is "who they are"	

★ 12 ★

Customer Problem Resolution: The 100% Principle

When it comes to serving others, chances are you will occasionally make mistakes. Even in the most opulent, 5-star hotels and restaurants, guests are sometimes disappointed. The same goes for hospitals, banks, nursing homes, spas, airlines, and any other businesses that serve people. The key to this seemingly unavoidable dilemma of making mistakes is how well you exemplify the "*100% principle.*" The *100% principle* is simply this: Whenever you receive a complaint or request, follow it through until you are 100% sure the customer is happy with the resolution. It does not get much simpler than that.

We recently had a new website built. The web designer offered a training session on how my team could update the site's content on our own. During the training, I asked about two features of the web software, and Kaci, who was the trainer, did not know the answer (she was obviously embarrassed about not knowing). She then promised she would find out and follow up with me.

Whenever you receive a complaint or request, follow it through until you are 100% sure the customer is happy with the resolution.

Now, over the years I have unfortunately developed a sense of skepticism whenever someone promises to follow up, because they usually don't do so. In fact, I am usually the one who has to follow up with the company who said they would follow up with me! Backwards...isn't it? At any rate, Kaci sent an email to me that same evening explaining she emailed the appropriate people and they would know the answers to my questions.

Note: You don't have to wait until the final resolution to communicate with the customer. Keep the customer updated on what you are currently doing to help.

The next day, Kaci sent me an email with the answers to my questions and followed up by asking if there was anything else I needed. She then proactively called me a few days later to inquire if we had any additional questions she could assist us with. Ladies and gentlemen, THAT was the *100% principle* in action.

At a recent hotel stay, I noticed I had forgotten my toothpaste and toothbrush at home, so I called the operator to request a complimentary set of those toiletries to be sent to my room. The operator said she would have it sent up within 10 minutes. 30 minutes went by, and still no toiletries. I then called back the operator to see what was going on.

Note: Your customers should NEVER have to follow up with you first. You should proactively give updates.

She said, "I thought THEY sent it up already." <u>I immediately thought, "who exactly is they?"</u> She then promised me the toiletries would be in my room shortly. Still, I received nothing 15 minutes afterwards. I then stepped into the hallway, saw a housekeeper, and politely requested toiletries from her cart, which she happily gave to me. Thirty minutes after receiving the toiletries from the housekeeper, I finally received the toiletries promised to me over 1 hour prior from the operator. That is NOT the *100% principle* in action.

The operator could have given me a time quote, and then followed up with the appropriate department to ensure the items were delivered. She could have then followed-up with me to either update me on the status or confirm I received the toiletries. The most important element of the *100% principle* is to take personal ownership of a request or complaint. Those who <u>work like they work own it</u> will follow through to the end.

Problem Resolution Follow-Up Log

Here is a simple follow-up log that you can use with your team. Please benchmark it, and refine as you see fit.

Date	Time	Request or Complaint	Forwarded to (if applicable) [Dept. or Person]	Follow-up with appropriate Dept. or Person (if applicable) [Date & Time]	Follow-up with customer [Date & Time]	100% happy customer? [Yes or No]

There are countless examples of people not following through. If you say you will do something, do it! Or at least make sure it gets done. Follow-up with whomever you need to, but your ultimate goal is to ensure your customers are 100% happy with the resolution. Follow-up, follow-up, and follow-up some more. Your customers deserve it.

Supplemental Section:

Whenever you receive a complaint or a request, here is a recommended sequence to follow:

1. Say you will own the complaint / request. Get the customer's contact information (email and phone # should suffice).
2. Get the customer's preferred mode of contact (email, text, phone call).
3. Begin the process of fixing the issue. Ensure the resolution matches the complaint / request.
4. If you need to pass the issue to another person / department to handle, then do so. (But remember, YOU still own it!).
5. Proactively inform the customer on the status every 24 hours using the customer's preferred mode of contact.
6. When you've received confirmation the issue has been resolved, contact the customer to inform them.
7. Follow-up to ensure the customer is, in fact, happy with the resolution.

Recommended tools for up-and-coming and veteran "follow-up" pros:

* Use a Problem Resolution Follow-Up log.
* Schedule follow-up reminders in your own calendar (use a program like Microsoft Outlook or any other calendar tool).
* Always demonstrate a personal attitude of ownership and commitment to follow-through.

Activity – Customer Problem Resolution – the 100% Principle

This activity helps put into place the disciplined habit of owning each customer problem from start to finish.

Instructions

Implement the Problem Resolution Follow-Up process on page 53 for your position and/or team...

1. Customize the provided follow-up log template to meet the needs of your team/company.
2. Say you will own each complaint / request. Get the customer's contact information (email and phone # should suffice).
3. Get the customer's preferred mode of contact (email, text, phone call).
4. Begin the process of fixing the issue. Ensure the resolution matches the complaint / request.
5. If you need to pass the issue to another person / department to handle, then do so. (But remember, that YOU still own it!).
6. Proactively inform the customer on the status every 24 hours using the customer's preferred mode of contact.
7. When you've received confirmation that the issue has been resolved, then contact the customer to inform them.
8. Follow-up to ensure the customer is, in fact, happy with the resolution.
9. Continue this process...check at the end of applicable reporting cycles (customer service feedback scores, etc.) to see progress made in...
   ◆ problem resolution and follow-up skills
   ◆ customer satisfaction scores
10. Recognize and reward excellence in problem resolution
11. Coach and redirect as needed to ensure problem resolution and follow-up are 100% to the customer's satisfaction

★ 13 ★

The Best Service School

Many people believe the perfect place to learn about how to provide world-class service is in a luxury hotel or a renowned hotel school. While that may be true in some cases, I found another and perhaps even more powerful training ground. On a recent trip to Charlotte, North Carolina, I saw and heard about service so memorable, it prompted me to ponder... "What if every person hired to serve others must first spend one-week training at a hospice?" Yes, you just read correctly...a HOSPICE. For those who do not know, a hospice and palliative care facility is a place that specializes in easing the distress and discomfort of a dying or chronically ill patient. Those ladies and gentlemen who choose to devote their professional lives to serving patients and their families in such a potentially traumatic time give perhaps, one of the most vivid examples of what engaging service looks like in its purest form.

One hospice executive said it best, "It is an ultimate privilege to take care of others. We don't get a second chance. We MUST do everything right the first time." I was fortunate to tour the **Levine and Dickson Hospice House** in Huntersville, NC. Like a luxury hotel, everything looked and felt exceptional. The furniture was exquisitely staged, the artwork was eye-catching and there was absolutely no clutter to be found anywhere. Most noticeable, however, was how happy, focused and professional the staff was.

"It is an ultimate privilege to take care of others. We don't get a second chance. We MUST do everything right the first time."

From the nurses to the housekeepers, to the receptionist...everyone beamed with immense pride. They were proud they were "called" to serve others. For them, they don't have *jobs*, they have a deeper sense of purpose to humbly and happily be hospitable. There is no such thing as *no*. As long as the patients and family's request is clinically and morally permissible, the team will find a way to make it happen. *Isn't that what world-class service is truly about?*

One employee happily recalled a recent stay of a terminally ill boy who wanted to see a fire truck. The staff eagerly surprised him with a visit from the local fire department and one of their big, red shiny fire trucks. Another patient had a craving for a vanilla milkshake with fresh strawberries. So the nursing assistant went out and bought the milkshake for the patient. Another couple in the hospice had been living together for several years, but never got married. The couple's interdisciplinary care team organized a wedding ceremony, complete with a chaplain, held in the couple's room. Those are just a few out of many stories shared with me.

"There is no such word as "no." As long as the…request is clinically and morally permissible, the team will find a way to make it happen."

Although I heard many examples of great service provided to patients, I was also the recipient of engaging service. Hospice & Palliative Care – Charlotte Region hired me to deliver a keynote session for one of their semi-annual all-staff meetings. The audio/visual coordinator loaned me his remote control handheld mouse to advance my PowerPoint slides. Before I began my presentation, I asked him about the remote mouse's brand because I was interested in getting one for myself. At the end of my session, he gave me a note with the full name and model number of the mouse, along with a website where I could buy it. He even wrote his email address if I had additional questions.

Also, since I was going back to the airport after my presentation, one employee gave me a small brown paper bag filled with snacks that I could take on the plane with me. She even wrote "Happy Trails!" on the bag.

…there is nothing more powerful than one person finding joy in being able to serve someone else

I often wonder when everyone in the service business will realize service is not about specific tasks you do in a job, but rather, a way of thinking and living. *If the purpose is understood, then the functions will take care of themselves.* In my view, there is nothing more powerful than one person finding joy in being able to serve someone else. We can all learn from hospices and the purity behind the service spirit that hospice employees have.

If everyone had to fully depend and rely on someone else to take care of them at some point in their lives, the true meaning of "service" might be fully understood by all.

Activity – The Best Service School

This activity helps bring focus to the meaning and actions behind "engaging" service. It requires stepping back and looking at your entire daily functions through the eyes of your customer.

Instructions

1. What does "engaging service" look like (from the eyes of your customer) at each point in the service experience? This includes every possible interaction (personal or functional e.g., facilities) with the customer…from the parking lot / landscaping to the back door / back dock.

_____

_____

_____

_____

_____

_____

2. What is your current reality?

_____

_____

_____

_____

_____

3. What must you do (personally, developmentally, in terms of accountability, etc.) to bridge the gap between your reality and engaging service?

_____

_____

_____

_____

_____

_____

Activity – From "Satisfied" to "Very Satisfied"

This activity uses the touch points identified in chapter 9 to help identify the behavioral differences between "4" *Satisfied,* and "5" *Very Satisfied.*

Instructions

1. Meet with each member or functional group within your team.
2. Use the activity from Chapter 2 (page 9) to help explain the difference between delivering a "Satisfied" and "Very Satisfied" experience.
3. Referencing the touch points list developed in chapter 9, work with your team to identify each touch point that helps deliver a "Satisfied" experience. Next, identify the touch points that help deliver a "Very Satisfied" experience.

   Note: Most, if not all of the touch points listed will likely help deliver a "Satisfied" experience.
4. Using the table below, work together to identify as a team, behaviors and actions you can employ to elevate each touch point to be a "Very Satisfied" experience.

Touch point That Delivers a "4" (Satisfied –meets expectations)	Behaviors/Actions That Elevate to "5" (Very Satisfied – exceeds expectations)

★ 14 ★

Take Your Service to the Next Level:
Only BIG WOW's...no bow wows

At a recent meeting, I was helping a team of executives brainstorm ways to WOW their customers. Once we began brainstorming, it became clear to me the mine and executives' perception of what a WOW was were completely different. To them, consistently smiling and greeting a customer was a WOW. To me, that is just the bare minimum of doing one's job in the service business. I then explained and gave several examples of what a true WOW should look like. I further pressed on by stating that they should only strive for the big WOW's. Then one executive immediately chimed in and said, "So, we only want the BIG WOW's...and no bow-wows." I literally could not stop laughing after I heard that one...hence, the title of this chapter.

Wowing your customers is just another way of saying, 'exceed your customers' expectations,' or 'create exceptional memories,' or 'provide an unforgettable experience.' At the end of the day, all customers want to feel valued, appreciated, and cared for. The challenge, in many cases, is for leaders to properly articulate to their team what a BIG WOW truly is. Of course, this also assumes the leaders, themselves, know what a WOW is.

One of the best ways of explaining a WOW is to begin by giving concrete examples. On a recent stay at an Embassy Suites Hotel, I decided to join their guest rewards program, which is called Hilton Honors. I figured since I would be staying in that particular hotel multiple times over a span of five months, I should take advantage of their rewards program.

> *Wowing your customers is just another way of saying, 'exceed your customers' expectations,' or 'create exceptional memories,' or 'provide an unforgettable experience."*

So I called the Hilton Honors' toll-free number with the single expectation of joining the Hilton Honors program. I was not prepared for what was to come.

Julia P., the customer care representative, not only registered me seamlessly, but she helped me get points from my last hotel stay, which qualified me for several thousand points. I did not know that it was even possible to get retroactive points!

Double Platinum Rule = yes   **BIG WOW = yes**   **bow-wow = no**

Julia then enrolled me in Hilton Honors' current promotion (at the time), which gave me a minimum of double points and a maximum of quadruple points based on length of stay.

Double Platinum Rule = yes   **BIG WOW = yes**   **bow-wow = no**

When I thanked her for all the insider information on the special promotions, she told me "I always tell my customers about our special promotions." Notice the use of the words *my* and *our*. Julia was obviously proud of her company and it showed.

Work Like You Own It = yes   **Service Ambassador = yes**   **bow-wow = no**

Julia ended the registration process with a genuine "Thank you for choosing Hilton Honors! We look forward to serving you again." The WOW's didn't stop there. I called back shortly thereafter because I forgot to ask a question about the program, and this time the customer care representative's name was Rich A. After answering my question, he immediately saw I had just become a new member. He also noticed I did not receive my new member bonus points worth 2500 points. Again, the Hilton Honors customer care representatives gave me things I did not even know existed! So Rich offered to insert those points into my profile a.s.a.p.

Double Platinum Rule = yes   **BIG WOW = yes**   **bow-wow = no**

Rich then went on to explain the Hilton Honors "Double-Dipping" feature, which would allow me to receive both airline and hotel credits simultaneously. Who am I to say no to free points?

Double Platinum Rule = yes   **BIG WOW = yes**   **bow-wow = no**

Companies who are renowned for consistently providing exceptional service have only one standard, and that standard is to WOW by any means necessary. In iconic service brands, like Nordstrom's and Disney, there is

Only exceeding expectations will do. Good is not good enough. Excellence is the only standard worth discussing.

virtually no discussion about meeting expectations. Only exceeding expectations will do. Good is not good enough. Excellence is the only standard worth discussing. The first principle of working like you own it is to begin each day by asking, "How and who will I WOW today?" The key is to consistently strive for the BIG WOW's and leave the bow-wows alone.

Activity – BIG WOWsI

This activity helps service professionals develop a mindset that only the BIG WOWs are acceptable...

Instructions

Based on our most recent work together, we now know what a "5" experience looks like. Our next step in taking your service to the next level is to work through what the BIG WOW's look like...

Complete this activity with your supervisor first...and if applicable, brainstorm possibilities with your team...

1. Think through the "5" experiences you have delivered recently...those for which you are most proud.
2. Think through recent "bow wow" experiences, as well. This includes any experience that would score a "4" or below on the satisfaction scale.
3. Now...what more can you do in the future, to turn or elevate those experiences to a BIG WOW for your customers?
   - Let's begin with the end in mind...What results do you anticipate?
   - What attitudes must you change?
   - What actions / behaviors must you employ?
   - What resources can you use?

Special Section

★ LEAD LIKE YOU OWN IT! ★

★ 15 ★

5 Stars vs. 4 Stars:
What's the difference?

Championship winning coaches have a habit of demanding excellence from everyone on their team. They never tolerate mediocrity from anyone. Incredibly high standards are discussed everyday (yes, *everyday*). This chapter, however, is not about sports. Nor is it about AAA ratings, Mobil ratings, or Michelin Guide ratings.

It is about what separates very good from exceptional. I've had the privilege to work with 5-star hotels, restaurants, and spas. I have also worked with 4-star establishments. The difference between the two is like night and day. 4 star properties are reputable and very good. In most cases, the staff knows what they are supposed to do, and they even have an idea about what great service is. In a 5 star establishment, excellence is demanded from everyone every day.

In a 5-star establishment, excellence is demanded from everyone every day.

- Mistakes are always reviewed.

- Follow through is always done.

- The best employees are always recognized.

- Everyone works like they have a personal stake in the property.

To put it bluntly, good is never good enough...employees in 5 star properties strive to be perfect all the time. The leadership in 5-star properties always challenge their teams and themselves to get better. Being 5-stars is more about a mindset than it is about adhering to certain standards.

So what are the best ways to implement this 5-star mindset? First, recognize that 5-stars is not about an award or designation. It's about a mentality...a way of working...discipline...and most of all, a healthy disdain for anything mediocre. Whenever you find yourself thinking, "Well that's ok," or "It's not that bad," or "It'll be perfect next time," then you're drifting away from the 5-star mentality.

Let me be clear, you don't have to work in a 5-star establishment to have a 5-star mentality. I've seen 3 and 4 star establishments with the 5-star mindset. I've seen grocery stores and airlines with the 5-star mindset, as well. Five-stars is about excellence and striving to be world-class in whatever you are doing…*all the time.*

I recently stayed at the Wynn Las Vegas, and had a 5-star experience. One of the true testaments of a 5-star experience is how well the staff takes ownership and follows through. Shortly after checking in, I ordered room service. When the order came, the server was refined, yet very personable. She asked me where I would like the table to be set up, and I told her in front of the television. She then asked about my television station preference, turned the channel to the desired station, and placed the remote control right next to me. After uncovering my food and describing each dish, she asked if there was anything further she could do to assist. I had forgotten my lint roller at home, so I asked if the hotel might have one for me. She said that she'd be happy to take care of it, and I would have an update within a half-hour. Less than 15 minutes later, someone was knocking at my door. It was a laundry attendant with a silver tray and 3 lint rollers for me to use. By the way, the attendant also used my name and inquired about further assistance also.

Keep in mind these were the laundry attendant and the room service server. Those are not the highest paid employees, but their actions created a 5-star experience. The true test of a 5-star establishment is not whether they can create a single memorable experience. It's whether they can create memorable experiences repeatedly every day.

From a leadership perspective, one of the best ways to do this is to continuously solicit and share examples of memorable experiences. Every week, solicit examples from your team, or read letters submitted by past guests. Just make sure you focus on the level of service you want to see repeated.

Focusing on excellence will stimulate more excellence. Talking about excellence will stimulate more excellence. Rewarding excellence will stimulate more excellence. One general manager with 5-star hotel experience put it perfectly… "It is the small, simple, special moments that we create through personal engagement with each guest that they will recall when they return home."

To accomplish this type of sustainability we carefully and methodically select our employees, and then continuously train. It's not about the tactical as much as it is about speaking the language of the guest."

The true test of a 5-star establishment is not whether they can create a single memorable experience. It's whether they can create memorable experiences repeatedly every day.

The key to getting started on this journey is to become very clear about your vision for service excellence. Share some examples from various industries. Ask your team about the most memorable service they ever received. Most importantly, challenge everyone on your team to take ownership and follow through on guest requests all the time.

5-stars is not an award, it's a declaration to your team that good is not good enough; only excellence will do.

Activity – 5 Stars is a Mindset...

The greatest danger to a 5-Stars mindset is being satisfied with delivering a 4-Star experience. 4-Stars is nothing more than doing the right things consistently. This activity provides an opportunity to *consistently* elevate your service standards to 5-Stars by improving on the standards you set for yourself.

Instructions

1. List the "must haves" for delivering a 4-Star experience from within your role.
2. Ask yourself "What if...I elevated my standard to 5-Stars?" How would that impact my customers?
   - What would have to change about my standards and behaviors?
   - By when?
3. If you lead a team of service professionals, complete the template below first on your own. Then ask each member of your team to do the same.
4. Set time-bound goals with each person.
5. Consistently focus on, talk about, and reward/recognize excellence.
6. Observe the changes. Follow-up, recognize excellence, and coach/redirect as needed.

4-Stars "Must Haves"	What Must I Change to Get to 5-Stars?	By When...	Follow-up ✓

★ 16 ★

5 Star Leadership:
What Does it Take to be a 5-Star Leader?

Five-star leaders share many of the same qualities. One such quality is to

In a 5-star establishment, excellence is demanded from everyone every day.

believe their team CAN be great. If they are not great, they must ask themselves if the employees are incapable of being great; or if the leaders' low expectations are inhibiting the employees' potential to be great. Yes, low expectations promote average and low performance, while high expectations promote high performance. I've heard many managers of low-performing teams blame their staff for the teams' low performance. "Oh, we can't find good people," "we don't pay high wages, etc." All of those excuses are surmountable. I've seen businesses in the same city or even on the same street, providing the same product, hire from the same labor pool, and yet have vastly different service experiences. Most times, the only difference is the caliber of leadership in the building. I've even witnessed a 5-star hotel go from exceptionally high service ratings to mediocre ratings. The staff was the same, the labor pool was the same, the tools were the same…the only difference was the change in senior leadership. The hotel initially had a general manager who believed in the infinite potential of the teams' service ability and subsequently treated the team like world-class professionals. The subsequent general managers *did not*, and the hotel has not been the same since.

There are many employees who want to work for a leader who has high expectations and believes in them. I recently had the opportunity to stay at the Marquis Los Cabos resort in Los Cabos, Mexico. The entire experience was among the best I've ever received. During my 3-day stay, I never walked by any employee without them extending a warm greeting. Everyone was always eager to serve.

One day I asked the hotel's general manager to tell me one thing that keeps the service levels so incredibly high at the resort. Without hesitation she emphatically said, "Keep the employees very happy." That's it. As business leaders, you may have repeatedly heard the mantra before: happy employees lead to happy customers. But there was something different about what she said and how she said it. I got the impression that "keep the employees very happy" was not just a public relations or HR jargon. The emphasis in her voice and the intensity in her eyes made very clear that employee engagement is a top priority at her hotel. The Marquis Los Cabos general manager is convinced there is a direct link between high employee engagement and exceptional service delivery. Engaged employees lead to engaged guests.

One of the great things about benchmarking is there are many examples of how highly successful leaders are able to keep employee engagement high. Five-star leaders, who are able to build and maintain a world-class service culture, do so by keeping their team engaged.

These leaders:

- Always maintain high expectations of the service they expect to see (no exceptions!).

- Always believe that each person on their team knows that they are a critical part of delivering the service experience.

- Never allow a team member to give less than 100% effort. Five-star leaders know that one under-performing team member can jeopardize the entire team's momentum.

- Talk about "excellence" every day.

  Newsletters are commonly used to share "standard of the day," company mission statement, story of service excellence, and business results like occupancy %. Five-star leaders know that engaged employees are well-informed employees

- Reward excellent performance on a regular basis (usually daily).

- Are always an integral part of the on-boarding process (hiring, interviewing, and orientation).

The general manager from the Marquis Los Cabos personally meets and/or interviews every employee from the dishwashers to the front office manager. Many of the world's finest properties don't allow new employee orientation to occur without the general manager present to meet and greet the new recruits.

- Ensure the purpose of the role is communicated during the interview and on-boarding process (e.g., your job is *not* to open doors, it *is* to welcome guests and make each one feel individually cared for).

- Make sure everyone is fully aware of their benefits (Distributing the benefits brochure during new employee orientation is not enough. Use lunch & learn sessions, along with other ad-hoc opportunities.

- Continuously invest in employee development (this does not have to be a training class; it can be a book club, one-on-one meetings, mentoring, or cross-training in another department.)

Note: *Five-star leaders know employee development is not dependent on short-term financial woes.*

- Mandate everyone on the team serves each other with the same sense of urgency, excellence, and attention as they would an external customer.

- Work alongside team members when needed. One of my fondest memories of a 5-star general manager took place early in my career. My restaurant co-workers and I were behind schedule in getting a room set for a large banquet function. Out of nowhere, the general manager arrived with every manager in the hotel to help us get the room set.

I once heard a saying…if you must say that you are a gentleman, then you really are not one. Your actions should speak for themselves. The same is true of a 5-star caliber leader. Be a walking, talking embodiment of service excellence. Inspire your team with actions and words. Five-star leaders know that the delivery of exceptional customer service is only about 20% of the formula. The other 80% (employee engagement processes) are what truly builds a sustainable culture of service excellence.

Five-Star leaders know employee development is not dependent on short-term financial woes.

Know that your team can be great, and never stop believing in everyone's potential. That is the true mindset of a 5-star leader.

Activity – What Does It Take to Be a 5-Star Leader?

This activity helps highlight or create servant leadership accountability within your organization. True success requires placing yourself in a vulnerable position, you are sending two very important messages to your team: 1) "Your opinion counts." 2) "I'm willing to put myself in a learning role to ensure a 5-star experience for our customers."

Instructions

Make a copy of the assessment below and ask each person you lead to complete it based on the following instructions.

1. Using the rating scale on the right, write a check mark "✓" to rate the way in which your supervisor leads the team in service excellence.
2. Return the completed assessment to your supervisor.

1	Strongly Disagree
2	Disagree
3	Does Not Apply
4	Agree
5	Strongly Agree

5-Star Leadership Attribute	1	2	3	4	5
My supervisor always maintains high expectations of the service he/she expects to see (no exceptions).					
My supervisor believes and communicates to me the importance of the role I play in delivering the service experience.					
My supervisor holds me accountable to 100% effort and does not accept anything less!					
My supervisor makes it a point to talk about "excellence" every day					
My supervisor consistently rewards excellent performance (usually daily)					
My supervisor actively leads the onboarding process for new employees (hiring, interviewing, orientation)					

5-Star Leadership Attribute	1	2	3	4	5
My supervisor clearly communicates the purpose of our roles during the interview and onboarding process					
My supervisor invests in my professional development (training, book recommendations, cross-training, etc.)					
Everyone on our team is required and expected to serve each other with the same sense of urgency, excellence, and attention to hold as they would for an external customer.					
My supervisor makes sure everyone is fully aware of their benefits.					
My supervisor works alongside me when I need him/her to do so.					

★ 17 ★

Service Excellence: Inspect What You Expect

If we truly want to serve in an exceptional manner, then we must regularly look at service from our customer's perspective. It can become quite easy to get so caught up in the day-to-day operation of our jobs, that we unintentionally overlook simple service errors. We, as service providers, can become very focused on giving service, and forget it's all about how our customers receive that service. As I've stated before, service is not about what we want to give…it's about what the other person wants to receive.

> *Service is not about what we want to give…it's about what the other person wants to receive.*

On a recent hotel stay, I decided to order dinner through room service. I wasn't that hungry, so I only ordered a bowl of chicken noodle soup. The chicken noodle soup came as planned. The utensils were wrapped in a cloth napkin (as I've seen before in many other food & beverage operations). When I unfolded the napkin, however, I noticed a fork, knife, and teaspoon. Given that I ordered soup, the only utensil I could actually use was the teaspoon, which was not an ideal choice. A soup spoon or, at least, a dessert spoon would have been more appropriate.

The following morning, I ordered oatmeal and once again, I received the same utensils. This time, I asked the server to please bring me a bigger spoon. Do you think the server took note of my request and relayed the information to her boss so the team could improve the annoying utensil situation? Not sure…actually, probably not. Ideally, the hotel would have a process whereby a room service employee would call the room a few minutes after the food was delivered to inquire if all was well. That way, the room service team would proactively have a system in place to identify and address service errors before the customer becomes upset. Inspect what you expect.

When I placed the oatmeal order, there was an option for 2% or skim milk to accompany the oatmeal. What do you think the milk is supposed to be used for? You guessed it…to pour into the oatmeal. The oatmeal came with a glass of milk…not a mini-pitcher or some other tool to effectively pour, but a full-fledged wine-glass with milk in it. Of course, when I tried pouring the milk into the full bowl of oatmeal, the milk spilled all over the place. *Inspect what you expect.*

Upon checking out of the hotel, I told the front desk agent about the soup and oatmeal issues (she also happened to be the front desk manager). As we know, most guests don't complain, they just leave and don't return. Then they'll talk about you, write blogs about you and make internet videos about you. As a manager, regularly "shop" the service experience your team provides. Give feedback and make improvements daily. Teach your team to be quality auditors. Have them ask themselves, "What does my guest need in order to fully enjoy what I'm serving?" Encourage your team to solicit feedback. Review the collected feedback as a team, and then make improvements accordingly. You'll be surprised at how many improvements are quick-fixes.

Make it a scheduled activity to audit the customer experience. The same way you have budget meetings and manager meetings on your calendar, please place the service audits on your calendar as well. It is that important. When inspecting…ask yourself, "What are my guests seeing, hearing, touching, tasting and smelling? In addition to personally inspecting what you expect, another great way to capture the customer's experience is to intimately solicit feedback from your customers. Be sure to get a nice cross-section of long-time customers (ambassadors), not quite long-time customers and new customers. This is to get multiple perspectives. On a quarterly or even a semi-annual basis, schedule an informal meeting or conference call to thank them for their patronage and to simultaneously solicit ways to better serve them. Some customers are more likely to open up and be thoroughly honest via these types of methods than the traditional comment card system.

Make it a scheduled activity to audit the customer experience.

Regardless of the setting, service always boils down to someone being the recipient of someone else's products and/or services. Your guests deserve the best you have to offer every time. Tell your team that serving others is a beautiful thing. Having the opportunity and privilege to positively impact someone else's day is a gift they should be proud of giving. An anonymous author wrote it best, "No one is more cherished in this world than someone who lightens the burden of another."

Activity – Inspect What You Expect

This activity helps create self-directed accountability for service excellence, which begins with the leader and cascades to the team. Success in completing this activity requires an open, honest, and accepting team culture with the requirement that each audit is treated as a blameless learning opportunity to ensure lasting results that positively engage the customer.

Instructions

1. Using the touch points list from chapter nine, "shop" your team's service experience.
2. Place a check mark under the corresponding number to rate each experience. Use the rating scale below.

1	Very Dissatisfied
2	Dissatisfied
3	Indifferent
4	Satisfied
5	Very Satisfied

3. As you shop the experience, make notes of:
   - If applicable, actions or behaviors that made the touch point to a 5 – "Very Satisfied" experience.
   - Actions or behaviors that can elevate touch points rated a 4 or below to a 5 – "Very Satisfied" experience.
4. Discuss results with your team.
5. Invite each team member to "shop" your team's service experience and continue the results discussion over the next several team meetings.

Touch Point	1	2	3	4	5	Notes:

★ 18 ★

Building a Team of "Living It" Employees

Every team has three types of employees...those who are *hearing it, believing it,* and *living it.* My hope is that by the end of this chapter, you will have a firm grasp on which group of employees has the greatest potential to help the team reach its goal of being world-class. First, allow me to explain that the "it" in *hearing it,* etc., has nothing to do with one's competency or years of service in a given role. "It" refers to employees' level of commitment in their role, team, and organization. I am referring to how emotionally vested they are.

Let's begin with the *hearing it* employees. They basically have an "it's just a job" mentality. They come to work, do what they are supposed to do, take their required break and go home. These *hearing it* employees are capable of performing this way for long periods of time, while not contributing anything more than the bare minimum. As I mentioned, the "it" has nothing to do with tenure. So the employee who has been on the job for 30 years can easily be only *hearing it.* Also, a new employee who may be justifiably apathetic because of a horrendous past supervisor may also be only *hearing it.*

"It" refers to the level of commitment that employees have in their role, etc.

Over time, and with the right supervisor, that *hearing it* employee may move up to *believing it.* These *believing it* employees have bought in to the company's culture and enjoy their jobs. They understand the "purpose" of their role, team, and organization.

They do their job duties, plus more. Take note, however, that while these believing it employees are reliable, steady workers, they are not "star" performers...yet.

Star performers are the *living it* employees. These employees consistently come to work early and leave late. They look for ways to contribute more. They have a burning desire to improve performance...not only for themselves, but for the entire team as well.

They tend to be the informal leaders that others follow after the meetings have ended and the memos have been sent. These are the employees who actually create exceptional memories and foster customer loyalty through their exceptional service delivery. While the manager may lay out the strategy, the *living it* employees embrace that strategy as their own and go about the business of implementing the strategy. The manager relies on

These star performers are the "living it" employees.

them. In fact, these *living it* employees can easily do the work equivalent to three or more *hearing it/ believing it* teammates. They are that good!

Now that I have explained the three types of employees, allow me to ask a question. If your goal, as a manager, is to build a team of *living it* employees, which group would you spend most of your time focusing on? By focus, I mean who should get the most coaching, feedback, recognition, and developmental opportunities? Whenever I ask this question in my keynotes and workshops, most people say hearing it, then a smaller number of people say believing it; the minority of people answer *living it*. While it is true that focusing on any of the three groups will likely lead to improvement, one particular group will stimulate the greatest results in the shortest amount of time with the least amount of energy from the manager.

Here is a brief analogy to illustrate my point. The winner of the 2009 National Basketball Association (NBA) finals was the Los Angeles Lakers. They were the best team in the NBA, which is considered by many as the dominant basketball league in the world. On many occasions, the head coach, Phil Jackson could be seen giving additional instructions to Kobe Bryant, who is the Lakers' primary star player (*living it* employee). The same pattern is obvious during huddles, locker room talks, and practice sessions.

Why, on earth, would this legendary coach, who has won ten NBA championships, spend additional time with the player who is already playing the best? Keep in mind this player already scores the most points, leads the team in many other statistical categories, and is the unquestionable leader on the floor.

Why would this legendary coach spend additional time with the player who is already playing the best?

On the surface, this leadership approach of spending most time with the *living it* employees seems foreign to most leaders because the norm is to spend the majority of time with those who contribute the least. Giving most attention to the *living it* employees first, then *believing it,* and so on will require a major shift in how managers *manage,* and how leaders *lead.* This point has to do with a basic, yet powerful, concept that can revolutionize how you manage yourself and others. It is often referred to as strength management or positive organizational scholarship. Essentially, it means in order to get more of what is right, then you should focus on what is right. If you want excellent performance, then talk about excellent performance. If you want more employees to exceed customer expectations, then talk about exceeding customer expectations.

Focusing on those employees who underperform only sends the message that underperformance, not excellence, is your focus. One of the fastest ways to de-motivate your *living it* employees is to accept underperformance or mediocre performance from everyone else. Your *living it* employees yearn to work for a manager who demands excellent performance. They go from job to job hoping this manager will finally be the one who models excellent performance, talks about excellent performance, rewards excellent performance, and chastises anything other than excellent performance. These *living it* employees want to be empowered and they want you to ask for their opinions.

An interesting point, however, is that *living it* employees will often tell you they don't need any extra recognition, they are self-motivated, and they don't require anything further from you. Don't believe them! It is not true. Read the following very carefully.

Everyone who works hard craves appreciation and recognition. They want...no...they **need** to know their hard work and dedication are being appreciated.

If the *living it* employees do not feel appreciated, they will either quit and leave, or quit and stay. Neither option is desirable. One key takeaway after reading this chapter is to rehire your living it employees. By rehire, I mean to spend some one-on-one time with your *living it* employee (or employees).

Ask questions such as:

◆ What motivates you?

◆ How do you (or would you) like to be recognized?

◆ From whom do you like to receive recognition? (they may prefer recognition from their customers or from co-workers)

◆ Do you prefer public or private recognition?

◆ What are your personal / professional goals?

◆ What are your hobbies / special interests?

Please understand this approach does not mean you should ignore your *hearing it* and *believing it* employees. This approach emphasizes that before you do anything else, make sure those employees who are contributing the most (your *living it* folks) stay motivated, recognized, challenged, and involved. It is much more catastrophic for the *living it* person to become de-motivated than if the *hearing it* person becomes demotivated.

Unfortunately, far too many managers over-utilize and under-appreciate their *living it* employees. In fact, there are many *hearing it* and *believing it* employees who, at some point, were *living it*. They are just waiting for their manager to focus on excellent performance and be consistent about demanding excellent performance. *Living it* employees take exceptional pride in their work and it hurts when anything less than excellence is demanded from everyone on the team. Here is a quick management self-assessment:

◆ Do I meet with my *living it* employees at least once per month (to discuss their personal/professional goals, their strengths, their areas for improvement, the department's goals, and the company's goals)?

◆ Have I recognized them for excellent work (over the last one to two weeks)?

- Have I personalized the recognition for them?

- Have I solicited their input on anything (over the last one to two weeks)?

- Have I used them to help recruit and/or interview any new employees? (Who better to identify and help select more *living it* employees than your current *living it* employees?)

- Do they have the appropriate tools and resources to do the best job they can?

If you want to attract *living it* employees, then BE a manager who values *living it* employees. Become known for valuing excellence and treating your best the way they deserve to be treated. Excellent companies who are revered for excellent performance have a large number of excellent employees. Focusing on excellence breeds more excellence.

Living it employees breed more *living it* employees. Therefore, I urge you to self-assess and re-dedicate your entire team to the one standard that matters most: Excellence.

Activity – Building a Team of "Living It" Employees

Setting and demonstrating the "Living It" standard helps communicate the expectations to every member of your team. It lets them know:

- You will spend your time where it gets the most traction… with your *"living it"* employees
- What it takes to get more time/coaching with you

Instructions

1. Spend some time evaluating where each employee is on the "living it" scale:
   - Who are your "Hearing it" employees?
   - Who are your "Believing it" employees?
   - Who are your "Living it" employees?

2. Answer the questions below to assess where you are in terms of leading your "Living It" employees:

Questions	Y	N
Do I meet with my "Living It" employees at least once per month (to discuss their personal/professional goals, their strengths and areas for improvement, the department's goals, and the company's goals)?		
Have I recognized them for excellent work (over the last one to two weeks)?		
Have I personalized the recognition for them?		
Have I solicited their input on anything (over the last one to two weeks)?		
Have I used them to help recruit and/or interview any new employees? (Who better to identify and help select more living it employees than your current living it employees?)		
Do they have the appropriate tools and resources to do the best job they can?		

3. Plan one-on-one conversations FIRST with each of your "Living It" employees to learn:
   - What motivates you?
   - How do you (or would you) like to be recognized?
   - From whom do you like to receive recognition? (they may prefer recognition from their customers or co-workers)
   - Do you prefer public or private recognition?
   - What are your personal goals?
   - What are your professional goals?
   - What are your hobbies/special interests?
4. Once you gain understanding of what motivates them, begin acting on that knowledge.
5. Next, have one-on-one meetings with each of your "Believing It," and then "Hearing It" employees.
   - Thank them for their contributions.
   - Let them know you want to work with them as they continue toward excellence.
   - Communicate your plans for your "Living It" employees and why you'll be spending more time with them (coaching and leading).
   - Share that it will them becoming a "Living It" employee take to become a part of that elite group.
   - Let them know steps they can take to get there…and they can get more coaching from you on how to become a "Living It" employee.

★ 19 ★

Service Superstars:
Treat Them Like They Own It!

"The trouble with having employees is that eventually you have to pay them." Wow! I heard a manager make that comment not too long ago, and I had to look at him to see if he was serious. Unfortunately, he was. In *Chapter 1,* we discussed the ownership mentality, which basically means regardless of your job title you should approach it with zeal, commitment, and pride. One thing I did not explain, however, is if you are a manager, and you want your staff to work like they own it, then you have to treat them like they own it.

Service superstars who work like they own it need to be empowered, informed, challenged, involved, motivated, and appreciated. The most difficult one for many managers to effectively implement is to make their staff feel empowered. Allow me to give an example. Often times when I travel on business, I rent a car with a GPS unit.

> *Service Superstars who work like they own it need to be empowered, informed, challenged, involved, motivated, and appreciated.*

Usually, I have no problems with the GPS units, but on two separate occasions the GPS led me to multiple dead-end roads and gave me outdated routes. Basically, the units had not been recently updated. At Rental Car Agency A, when I returned the car I informed the agent about my GPS problems, and she promptly:

1. Apologized (I'm so sorry for the inconvenience.)
2. Empathized (I can only imagine how frustrating that must have been.)
3. Fixed it (I'll go ahead and remove the GPS charge. I apologize, once again, for the inconvenience.)

That employee obviously was empowered (i.e., trusted to make decisions), and it showed!

Now let's contrast my experience at Rental Car Agency A with Rental Car Agency B. When I returned the car, and told the Agency B agent about the GPS problem, she promptly replied, "Well, that's not possible, they were just updated last month!" Then, she followed it up with, "Are you sure that YOU didn't do something wrong?" For good measure, she ended with, "Well, I can't do anything about that, so you'll have to go see a desk agent." In all, it took me speaking with three different people over the course of two days to get the stupid GPS charge removed. Now, which agency do you think I will use in the future, and which one do you think I will avoid?

Please note the employees at Agency B did not necessarily set out each day to ruin their company's reputation. They obviously were not empowered to do anything about my GPS issue. In fact, they may be legitimately disgruntled due to the lack of empowerment. They may be saying, "I want to help you, but THEY won't let me do anything (Note: "They" is the managers. See *Chapter 10 Service Ambassadors* for more information).

Owners make things happen. They don't sit around and wait to gain approval for small things. I know many business owners who get very frustrated when a simple solution turns into a bureaucratic mess. Lack of empowerment (especially in a service business) kills morale and negatively affects the customer's service experience. So if you are a manager and are reading this, I have three words for you... *Empower Your Staff.*

> *Owners make things happen. They don't sit around and wait to gain approval for small things.*

But be careful...empowering is more than just saying, "OK, now you are empowered." It is a conditioning process. Here is what I recommend:

- Start with a clear standard describing empowerment.
- Make sure everyone knows the standard (No, one memo will not be suffice).
- Regularly (daily) share real examples of when you empowered yourself and other empowerment examples with the team. This builds competency by educating your staff on ways to use empowerment.
- Recognize when employees show they are trying.

When I was a hotel front desk agent, my manager said I was empowered to make decisions. There wasn't much else in terms of guidance or direction. So one day, a guest complained the toilet in his room was not working. I proceeded to "empower" myself to comp the remaining three nights of his stay, which was grossly more than the situation warranted.

What do you think my manager did when he heard about it?

    a.   Yelled at me until my ears were numb.

    b.   Told me that the room night revenue I lost would come out of my future paychecks.

    c.   Thanked me for caring enough to do something about the situation.

The answer is C. He then immediately followed up by coaching me on various options I could try in the future. If he had used A or B as a solution, my confidence would have been crushed and I probably would not have been in any rush to empower myself again.

Use every opportunity you can to engage your team to make decisions. If you really want your team to be engaged, then you will…

- Empower them

- Inform them

- Challenge them

- Motivate them, *and*

- Appreciate them

Imagine a team full of people who work with a vested interest. Sometimes the only key missing is for you (the manager) to treat your team like they own it.

Activity – Treat Them Like They Own It...
The Empowerment Journey

The handshake that seals the deal of employee ownership comes from the leader's decision to empower each person to break free from the "rules and budget" game and truly serve the customer. This activity is about leading empowerment...it's about answering the question, "what are you, as a leader, willing to do to help your team become service superstars?"

Instructions

Take the following steps to get your team started on the empowerment journey.

1. For each role on your team, write in the space below a clear standard that describes empowerment.
2. Spend some time explaining that empowerment standard to your team...this is your opportunity to spend quality time training and demonstrating.
3. Consistently share stories (daily) about times you have empowered yourself to create a 5-star experience for customers
4. Share success stories when team members empower themselves to do the same
5. Celebrate (share your delight!) when employees empower themselves; encourage them to continue to make a difference in the customer experience through empowered actions
6. If an employee overcompensates, thank them for their investment in the customer experience; positively coach them through appropriate ways to deliver excellence without busting the budget.

Role	Standard
Receptionist	Offer an umbrella to a client.
	Order a birthday cake or card to celebrate a visitor's birthday.

★ 20 ★

Work Like You Own It...2.0
Energize It. Recognize It. Celebrate It.

Not long ago, I visited a well-known department store to buy a few items. I was armed with a list of carefully selected items that were on sale. When I got to the store, however, I realized that I left the sales paper at home. So I went to the store's customer service desk to inquire about getting another sales paper. The first person I met said he was on a break. The second person I met said she was working in the storeroom and did not know about such things as sale papers. Finally, the third person I asked said, "Of course! Wait right here and I'll get it for you." He then ran (not walked) to a shelf behind a counter and ran back with a sales paper. He then asked me what I was looking for and when I told him, he did not just simply point the way. He escorted me to the exact aisle and shelf where the item I was looking for was located. Afterwards, he asked if there was anything else he could help me with.

I thanked him for his follow-through and professionalism, and told him two of his co-workers apathetically disregarded my request. He promptly said the following...and I quote, "Allow me to apologize on behalf of my team and my company. That is not the level of service that we strive for." Wow. I thanked him for working with passion, pride, and professionalism. *He works like he owns it.*

Encourage It

If you want more examples of your team working like they own it, the first thing you must do is encourage it. This means to regularly talk about what it means to work with vested interest in the company.

Regularly talk about what it means to work with vested interest in the company...work like you own it.

People who work like they own it don't just take up space on the team. The team is better because they are on it. These service superstars are the exact opposite of those employees who just do enough to get by...I call those types of employees, the "bare minimums"...or BM's for short.

You can also "encourage it" by soliciting examples of when employees have exceeded expectations. But, don't stop there. Share those examples with the rest of their team. Excellence tends to encourage more excellence. Some companies are known for having an entire team of people who work like they own it.

Zappos.com is renowned for their world-class customer service. A colleague of mine recently ordered shoes for her son recently from Zappos. After her son wore the shoes only twice, they began to fall apart. My colleague was rightfully upset, so she called Zappos to complain and get a refund. She was fully expecting the operator to be defensive. The exact opposite happened. The operator apologized, empathized, and thanked her for bringing it to Zappos' attention. The operator then stayed on the phone with my colleague and suggested she log on to her computer so they can both find another pair of shoes right then and there.

After finding another pair, the operator arranged to have the shoes shipped via overnight mail (complimentary of course). The operator also upgraded my colleague to VIP status. In my view, Zappos.com is a great service company that just happens to sell shoes. In like manner, your company can be known as a great service company as well. The key ingredient however, is to have a team of people who take great pride in their job and work like they own it.

Recognize It

"Recognize it" means to catch people when they are exceeding expectations and let them know you appreciate them for it. Your best staff (the ones who work like they own it) crave appreciation. They may not articulate it, but they NEED to know their hard work and professionalism are valued. If not, they will either quit and leave or quit and stay. Neither option is favorable.

"Recognize It" means to catch people when they are exceeding expectations and let them know you appreciate them for it.

Don't just give a generic award; rather customize the recognition to the individual. Remember, if you want your staff to engage their customers, then you must engage your staff. Find out what they like specifically. Personalize the recognition, whenever possible. If I enjoy going to the movie theater, then movie passes may be a great gift. If I enjoy a double caramel macchiato with skim milk and two dashes of cinnamon from Starbucks, then a gift card would be memorable.

Celebrate It

Make "Work Like You Own It" a company initiative. Even if you don't use the exact term, encourage your team to...

♦ "Own" their work.

♦ Contribute ideas.

♦ Identify opportunities for improvement, *and*

♦ Be a part of the solution.

People who work like they own it should be placed on a pedestal. At that point, the manager's main responsibility is to keep that person motivated. In other words, DO NOT de-motivate those employees. Encourage them, recognize them, celebrate them, then get out of their way and allow them to create exceptional service memories one customer at a time.

Activity – Work Like You Own It 2.0...
Anticipate Excellence

Leaders must think "Big Picture" to meet the demands of their day...serve the customer, lead the team, and mind the budget. Successful leaders will tell you that taking care of the first two priorities helps ensure the budget issues never become a real problem.

Instructions

Answer the following questions to help encourage, recognize, and celebrate when your team works like they own it!

- What am I currently doing that could be a barrier to encouraging my employees? Recognizing them? Celebrating their "own it" performance?

_____

_____

- What actions can I take to encourage my team to work like they own it? What behaviors can I demonstrate?

_____

_____

- In understanding my team's preferences for recognition, what can I do to meaningfully reward "own it" performance?

_____

_____

- How can I celebrate employees' "own it" performance when they share ideas?

_____

_____